CW00431561

CONTENTS

WHY NORTHERN SPAIN?

Before setting off for Northern Spain, we had never really considered the area as a viable destination for an extended trip, but my brother Ian had told us about a hotel he was to visit in the small town of Amares, near to Braga in Northern Portugal. Ian was visiting with his family, wife Olga and their sons, Kian, Dzamils and Alex. Ian and Olga thought it would be a good idea if we could visit them and stay at the same hotel for a few days. Ian and Olga were working at the time and so they were going to the hotel for a couple of weeks. On the other hand, Lynda and I were on a career break and so had all the time in the World to get there and back again.

We did not fancy flying into Porto because we had unlimited time and so decided that it would be more fun to get a ferry over to Bilbao or Santander and then drive right along the northern coast of Spain and then turn up, to move into Portugal and then on to the hotel in Amares, Portugal. We had never been to this part of Spain or Portugal before and so started to complete our research into the area. We discovered that the Northern coastal areas of Spain are known colloquially as "green Spain". Excellent from the point of view going to a scenic area, but not promising from the point of view of the weather whilst we were going to be there. The 'green' meant that it rained a lot more in this area, than in the rest of Spain, so we were warned.

The journey from Bilbao to Braga was going to be around 750 - 800 miles, following the coast, virtually all the way. It could be done in around 600 miles, by following a non-coastal route but that was going to be a lot less interesting. We decided that we would follow the coast around the top of the Iberian Peninsula and complete maybe three stops on the way there and three on the way back. The Brittany ferry destinations in Spain, of Bilbao and Santander, were familiar to us from previous journeys on the ferry and were perfectly situated to allow the full exploration of the northern coast.

Our research confirmed that one thing that we would not be short of on this trip was going to be nice beaches. Time after time we researched towns, where the beach was not even considered to be one of the main positive points of the town, yet the beach seemed to be absolutely fantastic. We guessed that the water would not be warm, being on the Atlantic but we would be going for two months over September and October, the two months when the water would be at its warmest.

So, bit by bit our plan came together, using Booking.com we were able to chop and change and cancel, rebook and alter the dates, depending on what we found from our research. We opted to stay out of the main town centres, instead opting for smaller hotels and B&Bs in the more rural locations. Our timescale was going to give us around a week in our six or so different stops on the way down and back plus a week with Ian and Olga in Amares and four or five days on the ferry and that would be our eight weeks sorted.

The options for the various routes, when taking your car down to Spain are numerous. You can go over on Eurostar or ferry to Normandy, the ferry to St Malo in Brittany or Roscoff. However, taking these options involves a very long drive. Whilst these are the cheapest of the ferry journeys available, you need to factor in that you will probably need at least one stop in France, and that of course will add to the cost.

For us, overall, the most convenient and most inexpensive option was Brittany Ferries down to Northern Spain. Brittany Ferries is a French company and they have a monopoly in the UK on passenger ferry routes to Spain. So, a pretty major ferry route, between two major economies, the UK and Spain, is run on a monopoly basis by a French company, how does that make any sense?

We have always found Brittany Ferries to be just about ok. They are not going to win any customer service awards but if you want to go to straight to Spain by ferry from the UK, there are no other options. So, for the outward journey, we booked an "economie" ferry with Brittany Ferries, from Portsmouth to Bilbao at the very start of September 2019. The "economie" ferry takes the best part of three days to do a journey that could otherwise have been completed in just over a day. The ferry has a stop at Roscoff in France to take on new crew but cost about 40% less than the "cruise" fare so as Lynda and I were very 'time rich' it would have been crazy not to have booked the cheaper option.

As ever, the beginning of September crept up on us very quickly, in a way that it does, when you do not have a job to give the days structure. By the time

August was ending, we were already fully prepared. As ever Lynda had overpacked but once I made it clear to her that she was going to have to unpack and repack everything at least seven times, reality began to dawn and she had a reawakening and decided to reduce the amount of clothing she was taking with her. For my part, I was taking two pairs of shorts and three t shirts, that was all there was room for.

Before we knew it, it was time to go. The journey down to Portsmouth was a long one and the ferry would depart in the early morning. Therefore, so as not to risk missing the ferry due to traffic, as normal, we would drive down the day before and spend the night down there before departure. I can not recommend this practice highly enough, it gives a relaxed start to the trip and takes away a lot of the risk of missing the trip. It will cost you around £80 - £100 for a room plus breakfast for two. If you opt for an out of town hotel, and look for deals, you will likely be able to source a really good hotel at a very low price.

We found a great deal at the Macdonald Botley Hotel, situated near Boorley Park, a little bit out from Portsmouth but we were able to be flexible. It was a good hotel and room only was £50 for the night. Well worth it.

Even the restaurant was half reasonably priced and we had a pleasant dinner in nice surroundings. The hotel is about a mile outside the local town. We had visited the hotel before and had walked into town on that occasion and had eaten at a pub in town, but this time we decided that we would stay in the hotel and have dinner and a couple of drinks.

The following morning, we were up early. We always get up early before a trip. The ferry was leaving at around 10.30am and so we had decided that we would have breakfast on the boat or at the ferry terminal, which had a small, but usually busy cafe/bar.

We checked out of the hotel at around 7.30am. The trip to the port was about 15 miles according to our sat nav and took us around 30 minutes in busy, but not horrendous traffic. We arrived at the port, just after 8am, around two and a half hours early. That might sound very early, and check in was not open when we got there but we were nowhere near first in the queue to check in.

As we had seen previously, people actually drove their camper vans and caravans to the port the night before and actually slept at the port prior to departure.

We stayed with our car, until check in opened and by around 8.30am we were checked in and in the pre boarding queue. We went into the terminal, which was not too busy at this time of the morning. We were able to get a table and some breakfast, before the masses arrived.

One of the positives of ferry travel, over airline travel is that it is less stressful. You feel that in the hours before departure that you have time to realise where you are and what you are doing. With air travel, you tend to be rushing here, rushing there, then 2 hours of stressful inaction in an overcrowded airport, then more rushing. Ferry travel is normally a lot more relaxing, not as quick but just more pleasant.

Eventually all drivers and passengers were called back to their vehicles. So, we rushed back to the car and took our place in the queue. Eventually our queue started to move. We went through customs and were flagged through, whilst other cars around us were held and searched.

We then joined the queue to actually get on the ship. Our queue moved slowly into the bowels of the ship. The parking in the ship was as tight as ever, but the staff were very skilled and before we knew it, we were parked up and taking our overnight bag up the stairs toward our cabin.

It was a bit of a struggle to be honest, not because of the weight but because in addition to our bags, we were carrying big fluffy pillows. We always take our pillows because, of all the equipment you get on a ferry, the pillows are the worst. They are the cheapest pillows you could imagine and taking your pillows with you is well worth the effort.

We got to our cabin and having travelled with Brittany Ferries, many times previously, we knew exactly what to expect. The cabin was small, the 2 beds on either side, hardly wide enough to hold a normal weight person, goodness knows how some of the people on the ferry, get by in these beds.

We went outside on the open deck, to watch the departure. Somehow setting off on a sea journey, has something that the take-off on an aircraft does not. We watched the departure from the deck, on a nice morning and were headed toward the open sea, past the Isle of Wight and out beyond.

The ferry was to be our home for the next two days. Life on board was ok, but not great. Hospitality is not a strongpoint of the French and nearly all of the staff were abrupt at best and downright rude at worst. The cafe on the open top deck was good with a really good beef stew and chips but the restaurant on the public deck is reputed to be poor quality and is definitely too expensive.

Coffee, tea and wine are served throughout the ferry and can be taken out on to the open decks at the back of the ship. Indeed, we spent many a lazy hour at the back of the ship, looking over the vehicle decks below and out to sea. As this was one of the first ferries, after the kids had gone back to school, and the prices had gone down, the ferry was very busy everywhere. If you did not get your place quickly on the back deck, you would be standing as there were limited numbers of chairs. We were able to secure our spots for the stop in the port of Roscoff, France and watched the old staff disembark andthe new staff board.

We were pretty well rested by the time we approached Bilbao in the very early morning of the third day aboard. As usual, we were going to have to vacate our rooms, about 30 minutes before we were to arrive and as we were arriving at 7.30am, we needed to vacate our rooms by 7am.

We collected our things and made our way out to the public areas. This rule is so that the rooms can be cleaned in readiness for the new passengers, but it creates a real problem. There are nowhere near enough seats available and so people stand around - everywhere. They block stairwells, emergency exits, everything.

About 20 minutes after arrival, the deck numbers are called out on the public address system, one by one and when your deck number is called, you go down the stairs to your car. You then wait in your car for a further half an hour or so, before there is the sound of clanking and the noise of engines starting and eventually, the cars around you move and then you can start to move. After the wait you emerge into the blinding light. You are then into another queue and then onto the huts with Spanish border police, who are efficient and pleasant. It took us no more than 15 minutes to get through and it was then out into Spain.

You need to be careful when exiting the port, there is a lot of doubling back on yourself and it is very easy to take the wrong turn. So, take your time, follow the signs and after a mile and a half or so, you will find yourself on the main north coast road.

SUANCES

Suances is a medium sized town in the northern Spanish province of Cantabria. We had booked to stay in the El Castillo hotel on a headland, not too far from Suances town centre.

We were due to stay for a total of eight days. Suances is around 80 miles from Bilbao, right along the main North Coast road. The drive took us around 90 minutes. The road was truly excellent, way better than a typical UK motorway, absolutely smooth, with hardly any traffic on it – once you got past Bilbao and Santander.

What we saw immediately was - that even now, just beyond high summer, this part of the country was aptly named "green Spain". There were spectacular beaches on one side and pine tree clad mountains on the other. The area was truly spectacular. We were navigating by our 'in car' BMW sat nav (not the most reliable) together with a Northern Spain and Portugal map, but also by a map book.

Getting to Suances itself was not a problem at all - we went straight there. However, finding the hotel was a different matter. The address did not seem to exist in the sat nav and by now the maps were a complete waste of time.

Our Spanish was still pretty limited and so after a series of stops to ask directions and getting closer and closer, all the while, we found the hotel. To say that El Castillo hotel, was located in a spectacular position is an understatement. It was overlooking two fantastic beaches, one directly in front of the hotel and the other off to the side, over the road.

We had booked a sea view room and hoped that they would allow us to check in early as it was well before 3pm, when we arrived. As it turned out, they were great. They spoke good English and checked us in immediately. We had been warned that there was no lift and when we got to the hotel, we saw why. The hotel is literally in the shape of castle and the ground floor serves as a reception and bar/ cafe.

The upper floors were reached by way of a spiral staircase, so lugging Lynda's case up there was not much fun. At least we were staying for a decent length of time and so would not have to lug it back down again a day later.

When we reached our room, we were very impressed. The view out over the best beach you have ever seen - was stunning. The picture window, in the room was pointing out to sea, the right way for amazing sunsets. Additionally, in a sparkling blue sea, there were surfers dotted around, not seeming to make much effort to catch a wave, preferring instead to chat to each other in a circle. It was all incredibly scenic. It would have made a great postcard.

The room was spacious, not modern but just right for the area, with wood everywhere, paneling, floors, everything. There was not a great deal of wardrobe space and some of our things spilled out into the room and so as usual for us, the room was a bit of a mess, but that somehow sort of went with the casual atmosphere of the hotel. We stared out of our bedroom window, over the surfers and sea below and having taken about a hundred photographs, decided that we would go out and explore.

First of all, we went to the beach directly in front of the hotel. It looked like a Caribbean beach. Golden sand leading down to the bluest water, with surfers and swimmers in the waves. This was a "wavy" beach, interesting with reasonable waves, not wild, but by no means flat calm, the rolling waves simply added to the scene.

One thing we did notice that gave a clue as to the conditions was that whilst there was not a cloud in the sky and it must have been 85C by the middle of the afternoon, every single surfer had a wet suit on. When we paddled in the sea, we discovered why they were wearing wet suits. The sea was freezing, we were going to have to toughen up when it was time for our swim.

After a good look around this beach, we explored the bars and restaurants overlooking the beach. They were nice and enjoyed great views, we would re-visit these at dinner time. After enjoying an afternoon drink at one of the bars, we moved across the road to the beach to the side of the hotel. This beach was wild and very wide and very long. The rollers really were coming in here and there were only really people on the beach and paddling, very few were swimming or surfing in the water.

Again, the whole scene was very impressive and the higher level of breeze on this beach was very welcome in the afternoon heat.

To the very back of this beach, were three bar/ restaurants - they were very pleasant but being on this beach were a little more exposed than on the other beach and were buffeted by the wind. The bars all had glass fronts, which gave great views over the beach and sea beyond.

We walked to the end of the beach and found that the beach was bordered by a river draining into the sea. It all went together very naturally and the beach was, by late afternoon, very busy. The tourists in the town were almost all Spanish, there did not seem to be any English, German or any other nationalities around, which suited us. Again, we had a paddle and if anything, the water seemed to be even colder on this beach than the other.

The day was beginning to catch up with us and so we returned to the hotel and tidied up a little, so that it did not look as though robbers had ransacked our 'things', whilst we had been out. We sorted ourselves out and went out for dinner at around 6pm. We had a drink in our hotel bar overlooking the sea and then headed into town to eat. We had been off the main tourist route in Spain many times and we knew full well that Spanish people eat late, very late. In our heart of hearts, we knew we were heading out too early, but hunger and optimism got the better of us and we thought we would find at least one bar or restaurant open early.

We did not find a restaurant open and if we heard the word "Ocho" (eight) once we heard it ten times and clearly, we were not going to be able to eat until at least 8pm.

Therefore, we moved back to the restaurant overlooking the beach in front of the hotel and had a few drinks before its 8pm start time for meals. When the clock struck ocho, we had the fish platter and it was fantastic. The Spanish red wine was superb also.

A good meal in this part of Spain is not super cheap, because it is a popular Spanish tourist destination, but a decent dinner will set you back around 10€. A local wine will be superb and will cost in the region of 1 - 2€. Even the 'dodgiest' looking bar has a decent chef, they have to, they are cooking for locals, rather than the egg and chips British and German brigades.

The following day we visited both beaches for the day and took the 9€ 'menu Del dia' in one of the beach bars, for lunch. We went swimming in the sea for a period and then laid in the sun for an hour, whilst the blood ran back into our frozen limbs.

It was a restful day and just what we needed after 2 days on the ferry and the travel down. That evening we found out something that was to stand us in good stead for the rest our stay. The bar/ restaurant on the ground floor of our hotel stayed open all day until 9pm and served meals ALL DAY.

I cannot say that the food in the hotel bar was the best in Suances, but it was good and very cheap and very local. The wine was of course excellent and the additional benefit was that we could eat, whilst overlooking an incredible beach, with surfers and the most incredible sunsets.

The area had the feel of St Ives in Cornwall and we often discussed what a similar quality and located hotel in St Ives would cost - £250 a night, instead of the 90€ we were paying. The downside of the hotel bar was that it was too easy to simply eat and drink downstairs, instead of taking the time and effort to sample the different bars and restaurants throughout the town. However, we were determined to be disciplined and in the main, used our hotel bar for drinks only.

Having spent our first day in Suances on the beach, we felt that it was time to start exploring the area. So, the following day, we decided that we would visit Torreleveja, about 10 miles or so inland from Suances and the largest town in the area.

Our car needed a rest and so to soak up a bit more local colour, we decided that we would use the local bus. The hotel reception had told us about the bus, it left from Suances town centre and went to the main bus station in Torreveleja every 30 minutes or so. So, we got up early, grabbed a drink in a local bar and caught the bus at around 9am.

The bus journey cost around 1€ each. The journey took around 30 minutes and there were only locals aboard. We always enjoy doing what the locals do and the journey was great, seeing the local areas and sights from a bus. We reached the bus station in

Torrevelega and found it to be basically circular. We parked outside and before we left the station area, went inside, to find out where we would catch the bus back to Suances. From the bus station, we went to the local market, which was within half a mile of the station.

The market was a bit of a mix between a local food market and a tourist market. It was a very large market but not that interesting to be honest. The food sections were ok, but the rest of the sections were pretty uninteresting.

We went for a look at the rest of the town and found it to be a typical Spanish working town. Not tremendously interesting but with its own charm. The bars and restaurants were 'very local' with no sign of any leaning toward the tourist trade at all. We enjoyed our time in Torrevelega and upon having a little time to spare in the station, whilst waiting for the return bus, noted that Torrevelega is the hub for buses all over the region and we noticed that from here you can reach Santander and so we agreed that we would venture to the city, during this trip.

On the following two days, we stayed local, found somewhere in the town centre that served a superb 'tostada y tomate' for breakfast and partook of a couple more menu Del dias for lunch (incredible value at 9€ for 3 courses and a wine). For dinner, we used our hotel bar for one drink and waited for the 8pm watershed to eat at a local restaurant. It was restful and after these two days, we were ready to take on Santander.

In the UK, Santander is a bank. In Spain it is a large city and the capital of Cantabria province. We could have driven to Santander, but we knew that the bus went to Santander, albeit with a change at Torrevelega and felt that it would be better to go by bus.

So, we set out early and walked the mile and a half or so into Suances centre. We caught the bus to Torrevelega and after a journey of around 30 minutes, we were in the bus station, waiting ten minutes or so for the next bus to Santander. The buses seemed to be every 15 minutes or so. The bus to Santander cost about 3€ but it was a much better bus than the local ones - it had wi-fi.

Indeed, buses generally were much better in Spain than they tend to be in the UK. They were generally in good condition and showed no evidence of the low level, mindless vandalism that blights many of our bus fleets.

People were universally polite and pleasant and even the surliest looking teenager would happily give up his seat for an elderly passenger. The buses used for longer trips seemed to universally have wi-fi, which is obviously a boon, but to be fair, so do many buses in the UK. Most importantly, the buses are enormously popular because they are subsidized by the local authority and so are very cheap.

By and by our bus to Santander was ready. We boarded and it was a very comfortable bus. There were quite a few people on the bus, but it did not seem crowded. There were from memory only a couple of stops but it must have taken around an hour from Torrevelega to reach the city of Santander. We were dropped at the main bus station, which was straightforward. We had never been to Santander before and did not know what to expect.

We were very impressed by Santander, not only is it cosmopolitan, with a really nice, almost Mediterranean feel, it has some superb city beaches and fine hotels.

For a day trip, you may wish to visit Sardinero beach, or the Sealife centre, or the historic buildings in the city centre. Either way, there are tourist offices at various points, especially along the waterfront and these are a must for a short visit, where time is at a premium.

We did not fancy a museum or sealife centre visit in the glorious weather and stuck with the beaches, city centre and bars. Before long, it was time to go back and we simply retraced our steps for the buses back to Suances. It went without a hitch. We really enjoyed Santander, I know it is a phrase I use a lot but there was a really NICE atmosphere to the city, very cosmopolitan and chic. Both of us said that we would come back one day.

After a couple more days of staying local once again, we were ready for our final trip out from Suances, but this time it was going to be different, we were going to have to go by car - there would be no public transportation.

The thing that you will notice about northern Spain, when you visit for the first time is how mountainous it is. There were pine tree covered mountains, reaching for the sky everywhere and these can even be seen from the coast road.

We had seen these mountains every day and so we decided that we would like to go into the mountains to view the scenery and perhaps have a day in a scenic mountain town. After some research and pouring over maps, we decided on visiting a town called Potes, in the mountainous interior of Cantabria.

The journey to Potes took us about an hour and a half. It was a journey through incredibly scenic country, the road winding between enormous montains. The journey was slower than we had hoped, the road was slow and winding and there were roadworks for virtually the whole way.

We got into Potes and it looked exactly as we would have expected it to look. Both the town and the scenery around it were alpine in nature, with a river running through the centre of town. We knew that there was not a great deal to do in the town, but it was good to just look around, have our lunch in the town square and see the churches and buildings.

The main thing we noticed from the town was that it was much more touristy than we were used to and consequently, much more expensive. Lunch for two with a wine each came to nearly 30€, which in this part of Spain, is a lot of money.

The shops sold local goods, mainly hiking and mountain based, which were expensive but different and great to browse.

We drove back to Suances and after a further day at El Castillo, it was time to move on. We had really enjoyed our week and a bit staying there. It really was a sad day when left, but as we were to say many times on this trip, we would be back.

TAPIA DE CASARIEGO

The journey from Suances to Tapia De Casariego could not have been easier. It was three hours along the main northern coast road. We even found the hotel quickly, when our sat nav excelled itself and took us straight to the location.

We were staying at the Hotel Panorama just outside Tapia De Casariego. As ever we got there well before the standard check in time and were prepared to wait to be allowed to check in. However, as we found throughout our travels in northern Spain, the hotel owners were great and let us check in straightaway.

We had booked a first floor room with sea view, shared balcony and breakfast. It was 70€ for the room each night and the breakfast was great. The room was good and the sea view was across a major road, but very nice.

The hotel was perhaps a mile and a half outside the town but all along the sea is a public pathway, known as 'el Camino' which is essentially a pilgrims path running hundreds of miles down the coast to

Santiago De Compostela, supposedly the third holiest site in Christendom. Whilst we were in Tapia, we would see numerous pilgrims making their way to Santiago.

Once we had unpacked once again, we thanked the reception again and headed out in the direction of town. We could walk into town by the main road, which was the quick way or make our way across the fields and walk down the coast.

Either way it was a good 20 - 25 minute walk into town. It would be wrong to suggest that there is much at Tapia, because there isn't. A few shops, a couple of hotels, a few bars and restaurants and that was it. What the town did have however was a fantastic local fishing harbour, with bars and restaurants lining the top of the harbour wall.

If anything, the locals in Tapia, eat even later than those in Suances. It was almost impossible to get anything to eat, other than the odd tapas dish, before 8pm. Often we would go out about 6.30pm, have a pleasant stroll, down into town and then plonk ourselves down at one of the harbour bars and then stay there for the remainder of the evening.

We saw no other British people whilst we were in Tapia, but the town did cater for tourists, albeit local tourists. So, there were no bars or restaurants selling anything other than healthy local food. Around Tapia there are fields of vines, sunflowers and all sorts of vegetables. The fields tended not to be fenced off in any way and there was pretty unrestricted access to all areas around the hotel.

On our first morning at the hotel, we took breakfast there. There were only two other couples staying that day, both of whom were Spanish nationals. The breakfast was great, as it was on each of the six or so days that we were there. There was juice and cereal, together with fresh fruit, tortilla, tomato and local sausage, together with coffee.

Before we started to go to the non-touristy parts of Spain, I was totally a tea drinker and never touched coffee. However, the Spanish do not really get tea and a few times when I ordered "te con leche" (tea with milk), it would come back as a tea bag in warm milk, which is absolutely disgusting. So, I started drinking coffee and still do.

Following breakfast, we went to the beaches, just beyond the main town and harbour. There seem to be three main beaches, which in a way were in fact a single beach, split into three by the rock which outcropped all along the shore. As ever in northern Spain, the beaches were truly spectacular, with golden sand gently leading down into crystal clear water. However equally normal for this part of Spain was the temperature of the water. It was cold. Perhaps a bit warmer than it had been at Suances, but cold all the same.

We were now well into September, but the beach was pretty packed, exclusively with Spanish families on the beach with picnics and even lighted barbecues, often with children of an age that really seemed to mean that they should have been in school. We never quite worked that one out.

After a day spent locally we decided that it was time to try further afield. In this part of Spain, buses were not as common as they had been in Suances and so exploring by bus was not going to be an option.

Tapia is in the Spanish province of Asturias. However just over the border in the province of Galicia is the strangely named town of Foz. Foz is virtually unknown to British tourists and certainly we had never heard of it before we went, however this is a full blown tourist town, with a full tourist infrastructure.

It is full of tourists but exclusively Spanish tourists. It has a modern town centre and just in front of the town centre is a long beach, which is bordered by a river running into the sea. We had a look around and it is all very pleasant. However, if you drive beyond the town and the main town beach, and continue west for a little while, you reach even better and more interesting beaches.

Anybody with even a passing interest in geology will marvel at the metallic look of the rocks behind these beaches. Some were like pieces of steel due to the tin content of the rock, whilst others were like nuggets of gold, seemingly due to the presence of copper in the rocks.

So, whilst Lynda had a lie in the sun and periodically, we would both venture into the sea for a swim, I spent most of the day on my own little geology field trip, looking for specimens to take home with me. It was a great day and to this point in the trip, the weather had held up amazingly well.

The day after we had been to Foz, there was much excitement around Tapia, because it was time for the annual food and craft fair to come to town. They would be in town for three days, over a weekend and being there, you got the feeling that this was the most exciting thing that happened in the town, all year.

Of course, the weather turned on the day that the fair arrived and whilst it rarely rains non-stop for any period of time in Tapia, it only fully cleared up after the fair had gone.

The fair was great, there were local food stalls and local craft stalls and the largest stall in the whole set up, was the bar. Whilst the bar sold every local drink imaginable, the primary item on sale was the local cider.

This was not ordinary cider but a very specific type of cider. You knew that it was a special drink to the locals, culturally, because of the way it was being handled and poured. Instead of just pouring it out of the bottle into the glass, the bar staff would hold the bottle of cider high in the air, at 'arms length' and then poured it, from height into the glass. I am not sure what good this did but there was a bit of theatre to it.

The cider itself did not taste great, it was very bitter but the locals seemed to love it. Indeed, despite the poor weather, the fair did a roaring business. We had a look around the stalls and they were interesting, local people displaying local arts and crafts. We probably went round each stall three times, whilst the fair was in town and tried the local sausage more times than was good for us. However, after three days, the fair left the town and everything returned to normal.

Virtually next door to Tapia is the town of Ribadeo. This town occupies two parts, each located on opposite sides of the river, which runs through the centre of the town. The town is built into the hills overlooking the river and is quite scenic in its own way.

We wandered around the town centre for a couple of hours one afternoon and found the town to have something of an upmarket feel. There are quite a few nice shops and local produce stalls. If the town had been any further away from Tapia, then it would not have been worth visiting.

Around 40 miles west of Tapia is a very traditional Galician town by the name of Viveiro. This is another town that is on the banks of a river as it meets the sea. The town is one side of the river, but on the day that we visited it was incredibly busy and we had to park on the opposite side of the river. It was in fact the first time that I was not totally happy with where we had to park the car, it did not look the best of areas, we had parked on the road and our GB sticker did not help. However, it was fine and the only problem we had on the whole trip, was when our car got towed by the police - but more of that later.

The town centre in Viveiro was very traditional, with tiny alleys and small privately owned shops selling everything from local salt to tee shirts. The bars were small and traditional also. The town was absolutely teeming with tourists, but as ever in this part of Spain, local tourists, once again there were no British voices to be heard.

After a lunch of tapas and a glass of wine, and a further period of wandering around, we went back to the car and made our way back to Tapia. For what was a 40 mile journey, it took a long time, before we even reached the motorway and it took nearly 90 minutes to get home, but it was worth it, Viveiro was well worth the visit.

When travelling on a multi stop trip, we had learned the hard way that, it is best to complete any long and tiresome trips toward the beginning of your stay and in the last couple of days, to stay local. Not only does that make the whole travelling scenario less tiring but additionally it helps with remembering the places you have stayed and preventing a whole host of places rolling into one - in your memory.

A constant reminder of the fact that the Hotel Panorama lay on the Camino was available to us in the guise of a constant stream of pilgrims passing through the hotel, always staying only for only a single night.

Therefore, we decided that as we were within a mile of 'El Camino' we would take the time to walk a few miles of the pathway. At Tapia, the Camino runs almost along the coast and serves almost as a coastal path. We therefore decided that we would head east, from the hotel, actually heading away from Santiago De Compostela, but as the idea was to experience the trail, rather than reach the destination, it did not really matter.

We began to walk. The views from the path were fantastic. We noticed at once that the path heading toward Santiago contained a constant stream of pilgrims. There was almost no point when we could not see people on the path, even when we got well outside town.

As we made our way, we were intrigued to see that there was evidence, almost all along the path, of hundreds of years of pilgrims taking the same route. Every now and then there were guest houses to house pilgrims. We stared through the windows of one and saw that the pilgrims were being housed in dormitories and in bunk beds. To be honest, they looked like student accommodation.

Outside these dormitories it seemed that every pilgrim had hung out every piece of clothing they had.

The amount of washing hung outside these places had to be seen to be believed.

We also noticed that many of these pilgrim's dorms also had ancient looking bathing areas attached to them. They had running water still running through them and seating areas around a central well, where the water was located. We wondered how many pilgrims, over how many decades had had used these facilities.

We had unfortunately got carried away with the walk and had forgotten the old adage that every step of a walk away from where you are staying, entails an extra step to get back. We had walked for approx three hours and so it was going to take us at least three hours to get back - probably more, allowing for fatigue.

We ate well that night and slept extra well. It was slightly annoying when the next day, the day prior to our departure, we found a pilgrim's hostel almost next to Tapia, within a mile of the hotel, which also had the ancient washing facilities we had seen on our marathon walk the day prior.

We were truly sorry to leave Tapia De Casariego, when the time came. We would heartily recommend Hotel Panorama and the surrounding area. It is friendly and welcoming. It is traditionally Spanish and as they have not experienced our lager louts in this area, we are not unpopular as we are in many of the British tourist infested areas.

The one word of warning we would offer, would be that you are probably going to have to alter the times you eat. You will not get dinner before 8pm, no matter what. However, it is much the same throughout traditional Spain.

SANXENXO

As we slowly made our way across the top of Spain, there came a point, where we were going to have to turn south, in order to turn into Portugal, in order to meet Olga and Ian, at Casa Lata, just outside Braga. The time we were required to turn south occurred on the 200 miles, nearly five hour trip, between Tapia and Sanxenxo in Galicia, not far from the Portuguese border.

We had booked to stay at the Hotel Mariola, for five nights and it cost approx 80€ per night inclusive of breakfast. This was the most expensive hotel of the whole trip and the first one to have its own pool, so on the way, we expected much.

As usual the journey was great, right up until the point where we left the motorway. The trip took us around 5 hours, a lot of which was spent on the painfully busy and winding roads off the motorway. The scenery was however the usual northern Spanish mix of spectacular coastline and pretty little towns.

After a pretty tortuous journey we reached the town of Sanxenxo and thought we had reached our destination. Regrettably not, our hotel was not actually in Sanxenxo but about 15 miles further on. So, on we went. Twenty minutes or so later, we arrived.

Unusually for this trip, we were after check in time - so no problem there. The hotel looked like a tourist hotel, pure and simple. There was a crowded pool in front of the hotel and the beach and sea beyond looked spectacular. We went to reception and checked in. The common areas of the hotel looked ok - just about.

When we reached our room, it was difficult not to be very disappointed. The highest room rate, we had paid had delivered the worst room. The room was basic in the extreme. It had the feel of a budget apartment. To put the tin hat on it, the front door would not close properly.

We reported the problem to reception, who were pretty good to be fair and immediately agreed to move us to a new room. The new room was equally basic, but at least the door closed!

After unpacking, for what seemed like the umpteenth time, we had a pre-dinner walk in the late afternoon sun, in order to see what the area and hotel were like. We quickly found out, ours was a package hotel in a tourist resort. However, and as ever there were absolutely no Brits to be seen. This time there were one or two Germans in the hotel, but nearly all of the residents were Spanish.

From our previous stops on this trip, we did not think that Spanish people stayed in hotels like this - but clearly - they did.

Bearing in mind the touristy nature of the area we were surprised that the tourist infrastructure around our hotel was so basic. There were not that many restaurants or bars, we seemed to be in the middle of nowhere. However, there was one restaurant that we particularly liked the look of, which was perched on a cliff, overlooking one of the beaches.

In the circumstances we decided that we would go back to the hotel, get ready and then come back. We knew that the chances were that there would be no food before "ocho" but as ever, we were optimistic and decided that we would return at around 7.15pm, the very earliest time, we could possibly see it being possible to eat.

We returned to the bar/ restaurant at about 7.15pm and were pleasantly surprised to see that not only was the restaurant open, but even at this early time, it was packed. Maybe we would be able to eat pre ocho - for a change. But no.

The restaurant had opened at 7pm but for drinks only. Food was not served until - you've guessed it 8pm. So, we settled down and had a couple of drinks, before the 8pm watershed. From the moment we sat down, it was obvious why the restaurant was so busy, the views out to see and over the beach below were superb.

It was interesting to note that whilst the cliff was a 150ft drop to the beach, it was hardly fenced at all, just a small timber barrier that would not have stopped an energetic two year old. As we waited for

8pm we speculated how if that set up was in Britain, we would lose a couple of kids a day over the edge. Why was it that the Spanish who take a 'laissez faire' attitude did not seem to be worried. Perhaps their idiotic kids die out early – Darwinism in action I suppose, whereas the British idiotic kids survive and end up going to Ibiza fighting and taking drugs. Just a thought.

As the time approached 8pm, the restaurant started up the barbecue, which was located by the side of the restaurant. This was a pretty rough and ready place. One lady was trying to serve the whole restaurant, all the tables for which were outside and protected from the elements only by what was effectively a plastic sheet roof and side sheets.

In order to lighten the load, for the serving lady, we ordered our food and drink from the bar directly. Both Lynda and I opted for the barbecue grilled fish. It was very good and we ate our fill before heading home.

The prices were more than we would have imagined for this class of restaurant. A nice glass of Spanish red wine was 2.50€ and a main course at dinner would have cost around 10€. These were tourist prices, but prices for Spanish tourists, not foreign tourists, which would have been a further step up.

The following day, as we always tended to do on our first day anywhere, we stayed local. We went to the beach which was opposite the hotel. This beach was different from the other beaches we had been to on this trip but in many ways the same.

As we approached the beach from the sand hills at the back, it was unbelievable- the sand was so golden and the water so blue that you could have been in the Far East or the Caribbean. One thing we noticed at once was that whilst the beach was incredibly busy, there was nobody in the sea.

We guessed why and we were correct, the water was freezing cold. It was difficult to believe but as we moved south, the water had become even colder. We did go into the sea and it really was cold, you could not stay in there for very long.

So, a day on the beach was periods of swimming, interspersed with other periods taken warming up on the beach after having been chilled to the bone. It really was odd, getting chill blanes from the water, whilst the sun beat down, without a cloud in the sky. We got lunch at a beach bar, but could only get a takeaway, as it was so busy.

That night we went to the restaurant on the top of the cliff again. It was a Friday night and there was a fiesta type atmosphere all around the restaurant. However, we were going to the weekend market in Sanxenxo the following day and so we had our usual couple of drinks and a nice dinner and then we left to get to bed relatively early so that we would be ready for an early start on the following day. As it turned out, I wished we had not bothered to go.

In the morning we were up early and were one of the first in the breakfast room that morning. The breakfast was not up to much but there was juice and so we were ok. We set off to get to the market early, when we guessed that the food and fish sections would be at their most interesting.

We would have got to the market at just before 9am. Even at that time the town was absolutely heaving. Parking was a problem, the roads of Sanxenxo were small with almost no on street parking. Eventually we found a car park. Parking seemed to be prohibited in the area in the afternoons but seemed to be ok during the mornings, so we parked there.

Our Spanish was not great, but we checked the sign time and again, put it through a translation app and it seemed ok to park there on a Saturday morning. We went off to the market and had a good time wandering around for a couple of hours.

It was a pretty touristy market, with a good mix of local goods and tourist goods. After we had finished, we returned to the car park, in order to collect our car. When we reached the car park where we knew where we had parked, we found no sign of the car.

It was a really odd feeling. The first thought was that we were in the wrong car park. But no - after careful inspection it was definitely the correct car park. We then thought that the car had been stolen. However, we had been very careful about locking it and if it had gone then they must have broken into the car.

We searched the whole car park, searching for glass but there was none to be found. Eventually it dawned on us, the car had been towed away. We asked a few people and eventually found out where the local police station and vehicle pound was.

We were lucky that the station was walkable, but we did not feel lucky as we made our way the mile or so to the police station. When we got there, we spoke to the front desk. Yes, they had towed our car. The policeman in charge spoke a little English and explained that whilst it would normally have been ok to park in the car park on a morning, it was market day and all bets were off.

Had this been the UK I would have complained bitterly about the lack of clarity, but in Spain, talking to an armed policeman, arguing did not seem a good idea. He made it clear that if we did not hand over 100€ we would not be getting our car back. Our options were not great, so we paid. It put a bit of a dampener on our stay in Sanxenxo but it did make us a lot more careful about where to park the car.

From Sanxenxo, the vast majority of the rest of the dry land was to the south of our hotel's position. So just for the day and shortly before we headed into Portugal, we headed north. We went across a small isthmus and to the end point of the area.

We stopped at a small town called Ogrove. It had a small harbour, which on the day we went had a small market spread along its length. There were a few bars and restaurants around the harbour and we went in one for lunch, having explored the whole of the harbour area.

After lunch, we decided that we would head further north and after a nice drive, we found a beach which was covered in shells, with a few fishing boats dotted around the water. It was not the most scenic place we had seen on our trips but was traditional and it was enjoyable to look around and see how life goes on in a small Spanish coastal town.

The final visit of this stage in our trip, was in retrospect a practice for our upcoming trip to Portugal with Ian and Olga. Sanxenxo, like most Spanish towns has a football team, which plays in the local stadium. From what I could find on the internet,

Sanxenxo plays in the regionalised fourth tier of Spanish football. Therefore, we visited their ground, which was coincidentally situated in the area, where the market was. I had noticed the ground when we went to the market, so we went to back to have a closer look.

Whilst in Spain, the 4th tier has about 40 teams and is completely regional, the ground was still unimpressive. There were almost no supporter areas and even the pitch did not appear in good condition. We would see much finer facilities during our next stop. Our five days were at an end and it was time to move on.

It would be wrong of me to paint our stay in Sanxenxo as anything other than slightly disappointing. Of the places we stayed in northern Spain this was the most expensive, most touristy and least likeable. However, the bar in that regard is particularly high in northern Spain and I really would not want to put anybody off visiting the area.

AMARES Nr BRAGA (PORTUGAL)

The border between Spain and Portugal falls on a motorway and to be honest, it was very difficult to tell when you were crossing it. One minute we were in Spain, going along nicely and then all of a sudden you are in Portugal.

Nothing changes immediately, except the road signs, but after a while of driving in Portugal, you realize that Portugal is a poorer country, the roads are a bit worse, the cars are a bit worse and the people look just a bit poorer.

By now, our sat nav had become accustomed to the Spanish and now Portuguese addresses we were entering and we reached Amares around two hours after we set off from Sanxenxo.

We found Casa Lata Hotel without much of a problem and immediately discovered that the hotel was in the middle of a vineyard. Once again, we arrived at the hotel, well before we were supposed to be checking in. However, once again the hotel reception was great and let us check in early. Lynda and I had a room overlooking the pool, whilst Ian, Olga and kids had rented the Villa, a self contained house in the grounds of Casa Lata.

We were staying for 5 nights and the price for the room, with breakfast for two was 80€ per night. As soon as we made it to the room it was clear that it was a very good deal,

Ian and Olga had been to the hotel before and so were aware of what was in the area. Casa Lata was not only a hotel with a vineyard attached but also had its own wine label. The hotel produced its own wine, from its own wine, on site. Because Ian and Olga had been such good clients and, in the past had bought a lot of wine, we were given a free guided tour of the winery.

We were shown where the grapes were juiced, where the juice was stored, the vessels where the wine was fermented and the bottling area, where the finished wine was bottled and labels. The wines produced at Casa Lata were slightly sparkling whites and light reds. They were excellent and we brought a case back with us.

Unfortunately, our route home was just as circuitous as our route to Casa Lata and we had allowed the wine to overheat and most bottles had spoiled by the time we got them back.

Each morning whilst we stayed at Casa Lata, before breakfast, Lynda and I would wander down the road, past the vineyard to the small bar at the bottom of the lane. This bar has the dubious distinction of being the least expensive public bar we have ever visited, anywhere in the World. Each morning we would have a coffee, a port and a pastel de nata (a type of small custard tart) each and the bill would be less than 1.50€ each. To be fair it was like visiting somebody's private house, but it was very cheap.

The pool was excellent, not the biggest but warm and good fun. Certainly, Ian & Olga's kids loved it. We went in a few times, but there were other things to do. The hotel encouraged you to walk through the vineyard and take a look at it. We did so on numerous occasions, and I would often try the grapes, it was approaching harvest and they were excellent. However, when the hotel pointed out that the insecticide used on the grapes meant that you should not eat many, it put me off them.

Whilst at Casa Lata, we took a number of trips to different areas and one of the very first was to Porto, the second largest city in Portugal. When we are in a city with a famous football team, we always try to visit the local football club and so we were grateful when we found out that Olga had arranged for us all to visit the ground of Porto FC, one of Portugal's biggest football clubs.

We were on the official stadium tour and were able to go behind the scenes, tour the directors' areas and executive seating, the changing rooms, the press interview areas and we were able to go down to the pitch and sit in the subs and coaches' areas. However, they did not want us to go on the playing surface. I got into the penalty box area for a few minutes but was told to go to the side. It was the start of the season and the playing pitch did look in great condition.

Ian and Olga were keen to show us everything in the area and so we went on a trip everyday, we were at Casa Lata. The hotel was away from the coast and if you were not going to go out for the day, there were only a few things to do. When Ian and Olga told us about hot springs in the mountains close to Braga, we jumped at the chance to go. We had been to Iceland a number of times previously and had always going to the hot springs over there.

The route up to the hot springs was very rough and whilst you could make it up there if you had an all terrain vehicle, we were in cars and so we needed to catch the bus that periodically went up there. We drove to a staging post, which had a lot of activities for kids. The kids had a climb and a play, which involved a zip line finish and eventually it was time to go up to the hot springs. We were taken up there in a pretty rickety all terrain van, which shook us to the core, all the way up to the springs.

When we reached the springs, we immediately saw that it was not as we had expected. These were not individual pools but a river, with lots of rocks on the bottom. We noted that the rocks had been arranged in patterns around certain parts of the river and people were congregated around those areas. We guessed that those were the areas around which the hot spring water was coming out. We found a suitable spot on the grass banks of the river and put our things down. We had our swimming wear underneath our clothes.

It was a boiling hot day but as we had become used to the water of the river was truly freezing cold. We immediately made our way over to the area where the hot spring water seemed to be coming out. It was not easy to get over and past the others but eventually we reached the warm water area.

It was warm and quite a pleasant experience as the hot spring water warmed the cold river water. The problem was that if the current was diverted by even a small amount, you were cold again and had to readjust. However, it was free and a good time for an afternoon.

At the end of the afternoon, we got the bus back to where our cars were parked. On the way back, Lynda and I were going to stop somewhere for dinner. Ian, Olga and the kids preferred to eat back at the hotel.

When we reached one particular town, which looked nice, we stopped and had a look around. It was very

'Portuguese' but to this day, I do not know the name of the town. We found a likely restaurant in the town square and went inside. It was only 7.30pm and so we were the only ones in there - of course.

Whilst having a pre dinner drink and a look around the restaurant we noticed that this was a religiously themed restaurant. The owner/ cook/ waitress told us that the restaurant was owned by a local order of nuns and all profits went to that order. It was a bit more expensive than we were used to but that was fine, at least the profits were going to a good cause.

The following day, we went to the ground of our local football Club, Braga FC. They were a Portuguese Primeira Liga side, but not one of the top Portuguese sides. We went on the official club tour.

The common areas, changing rooms and press facilities were a real step down from Porto, but the playing area itself was like no other ground we have seen before or since. It was explained on the trip, that the ground had effectively been cut out of sold rock. We were shown how it had actually been built into the rock itself. Large sections of natural rock formed part of the structure of the ground itself.

Most amazing to us was that this was a football ground with only three usable sides. One of the sides, behind a goal was sheer solid rock. It was as if they were still excavating and would make the area bigger as they got more time.

One of the positives of Braga FC over Porto FC was that they were not as precious about the actual playing surface and we were allowed on the pitch, as long as we did not act stupidly.

After the tour we went into the souvenir shop. Despite the fact that Braga are a top tier side, the souvenir shop was very small and had only a small selection of goods. We bought a little and then left.

One of Olga and Ian's favourite places around Amares was a river called the Cavado. It was a winding river and there were canoes and rings for hire so that you could float around the river. The kids had their own inflatable boat and had a great time paddling around etc. As ever the weather was glorious, but the water was freezing, but by now we were getting used to the constant contrast between the water temperature and the air temperature and it was nice to spend a few hours in a very scenic natural setting, chasing the fish around the river.

Like most of the places we visited around Amares the river was free to visit and very popular.

On the day before we left Ian and Olga, for Lisbon, we realised that whilst we had visited Porto FC, we had not been to Porto the city and that was a shame, bearing in mind the Porto is Portugal's second city. Therefore, we arranged to go to Porto. Rather than go into the city centre and wandering around the shops, which would have been no fun for the kids, we decided that we would go to one of the city beaches, that we had heard so much about. The day we went was bright and sunny as usual. As we got close to the city beaches two things became obvious to us.

Firstly, it was incredibly busy, the traffic leading toward the beach was very heavy and it was clear that a lot of people had the same idea, that hot Sunday afternoon. The second point was that we were going to really struggle to park. There were precious few car parks and whilst there was a fair amount of 'on street' parking, that seemed to have been largely taken, by the time that we got there in mid morning.

After about 20 minutes driving around, looking for a parking spot, we eventually found spaces around three streets back from the beach. That meant that we had to carry all of the beach equipment a few hundred yards to the beach.

It was not a big problem, just a pain. When we reached the beach, we could not believe what we saw. We have never been to Benidorm or any of those mass tourist resorts and so the sheer number of people on the beach came as a bit of a shock. It was immediately obvious that we should not have visited on a Sunday.

To be honest it was a bit too crowded for me, and so I went for a walk down the coast. It was incredible, the further I went, the more crowded the beaches became. The sheer numbers were incredible, and I would not have minded, but the beaches were not even that great! I wandered into town but most of the shops were closed. I have to say however that it seemed a nice city and the prices seemed a little lower than when in Spain and it was a shame that we could not have taken a proper look around.

When I returned to our group, I have to say that I honestly had a bit of trouble finding them, it was so busy. When I was having a sit down, I noticed that this was probably the worst beach we had seen. The sand wasn't great, it was stony and the sea was not totally clean and was full of weed, yet half of Portugal was on there.

One interesting thing from that day was the integral snorkel and face mask contraptions Ian and Olga had bought their kids. They looked really good and allowed the kids to breathe normally, whilst snorkelling. Our own kids were now adults but when they were young, they would have loved these. As ever the sea was freezing but the kids had wet suits and so loved it.

Whilst at Amares we saw most of what the area had to offer. It is pleasant and cheap, with some interesting places. Five days was about right to get a flavour of the place. The hotel we stayed at - Casa Lata was excellent, if it was situated by the sea it would cost twice its current room rate. However, all good things must end and it was time to leave Ian and Olga. It was time to move on to Lisbon.

LISBON

The journey from Porto to Lisbon was around 180 miles and took us about four and a half hours, with a stop. The motorway and A roads were good but not in the same class as the main northern motorway in Spain.

We were due to stay in the Lisboa Plaza Hotel in the heart of Lisbon city centre. This was a first class hotel and they had a special offer on for the over 50s and we paid less than 90€ per night, including breakfast for two, for the 5 nights of our stay. Unfortunately, the price was increased substantially by the fact that we had our car with us, and it was 12€ per night to park the car at a nearby location.

The traffic getting into Lisbon city centre was bad, but not quite as bad as it could have been. It was late September by now and we did get a bit rain in Lisbon and it was lightly raining, when we got there. We checked in and found the common areas of the hotel to be great. Our room was traditional in design, larger than you might have expected for a city centre room, with timber floor and wooden paneling, even in the bathroom.

The parking did not appear totally secure and so we had to unpack everything from the car to the room. It was late afternoon/ early evening, by the time we were showered, unpacked and ready to go out.

The hotel was located just off the Avienda Liberdade, one of the really major roads, through Lisbon city centre and so immediately we stepped out of the hotel, we were in the middle of everything. Our first impression of Lisbon was overwhelmingly positive. There was clearly a thriving cafe culture and within a hundred yards of our hotel were situated a number of permanent street cafes, which served drinks, together with a slightly limited food menu, at all times, not just ocho or later.

We were clearly going to have the luxury of eating where we wanted to eat. On the first evening we ate at one of the pavement cafes just in front of our hotel. The area was perfect for outdoor cafes, there were trees lining the pathway and dotted around the trees were pavement cafes, all down the road. The food was very traditional, there did not seem to be a lot of tourists around and the cafes seemed to be catering to the local Portuguese office workers.

As we were in the capital and in one of the most expensive parts of that capital, prices were higher than we had been used to on this trip, but nothing compared with what you would pay in London. We would have paid around 2.50€ for a glass of wine and 12€ for a main course. The quality was good.

We went back to the hotel, had the free glass of port, we had been promised in the hotel bar and went to bed. The following morning, we went down to breakfast, which was buffet style, except they would cook bacon and eggs to order if asked. It was generally excellent.

We had decided that it would be pointless to try to use the car as it was too congested in the city centre. We left the hotel and turned right down Av. Liberdade and headed toward the sea. Lisbon was very cosmopolitan. There were tourists and certainly quite a few Americans but as ever no British.

Having passed a number of really high end shops, about a mile and a half down the road, we came to a large square. It was a huge open space with a monument at its centre and with bars and restaurants along the outside.

The waterfront was on the other side of the road from the square. After a full look around and a lot of photographs, we headed over the road to the promenade, which ran along the waterfront. We walked along the waterfront, past government buildings on the opposite side of the road and past a park and a tourist area with bars and restaurants and on to what appeared to be a ferry terminal.

It was called Cais Do Sodre and faced another port, perhaps three or four miles across the water. We discovered that the town was called Cacilhas. We had no idea what was there or what it would be like but with a ferry fare of 1.30€ we thought - why not? So, we waited the ten minutes or so for departure time. It was clear from the people catching the ferry that this was a working ferry, our fellow passengers were not tourists and equally clear that Cachilas was not an upmarket place. These were commuters, working in central Lisbon and commuting to the suburbs by boat.

The ferry took about 15 minutes to cross the harbour. The ferries themselves was not a million miles away from the Star Ferries of Hong Kong. They were old noisy and two stories tall. As in Hong Kong it was a really enjoyable trip, feeling the sea breezes on you in the heat. When we arrived, we found the port to be small but pleasant. There were stalls and fish restaurants surrounding it and judging by the prices on the menus, it was a lot cheaper here than in central Lisbon.

We made our way into the town centre and to be perfectly honest it was not super exciting, but it was pleasant walking around a truly working class area. It was clear that the ferry was so cheap because a lot of people were commuting to and from Lisbon centre each day from Cacilhas.

There was little for the tourist apart from a plethora of fish restaurants, every single one of the serving sardines, Portugal's National dish. However, it was not lunch time and we had enjoyed a nice breakfast in the hotel, so we found a nice cafe in the heart of Cacilhas town centre and each had a coffee, with the largest pastel de nata either of us had ever seen. The total cost was around 2€.

We made our way back to the port, on to the ferry and then back over to Lisbon. We had heard of the Time Out Market, which we knew was close to the ferry port. It was early afternoon by now and lunch time. After a little searching, we found the market at the back of the railway station.

The market is not really that anymore. There is certainly a small market on the site. However, this is now essentially a pretty upmarket collection of bars and restaurants, with communal seating in the middle. We tried the fish, with a local wine. The prices were as you would expect when eating in an iconic destination - high. It was 15€ for a small plate of fish and 5€ per wine. Not horrendous but certainly above the norm.

We stayed local for dinner that night and were really enjoying our stay in Lisbon and the way we could actually eat a little earlier. We had by now discovered a small football themed bar, just around the corner from our hotel, they served great food, opened at 5.30pm and was reasonably priced. We enjoyed our dinners there and liked the casual nature of the restaurant.

It had not been long since our visit to Amares and we had been to two football grounds, whilst there. In Lisbon there were two huge football clubs, possibly the two largest clubs in the whole of Portugal. So, we decided that on the following day, we would visit both grounds. First thing in the morning we got on to the underground system and headed for Teleheiras, the location of the Sporting Lisbon ground. This ground was almost the length of the underground system away. It took about 40 minutes on the underground and a change of trains to get there.

Sporting are based in a very working class area of Lisbon. The underground drops you at a pretty dodgy looking shopping centre, across a major road from the ground. Everything in this part of Lisbon is green and white, Sporting's colours.

The ground is impressive in terms of its size but, looks a little tired. We took the stadium tour and found this to be very tightly controlled and not very inspiring. It was a little difficult to warm to Sporting, they were very much a local team and did not really pander to the visitor, in the way that Porto and Benfica did.

A couple of points to be made about travel and safety would be appropriate here. With regard to travel, you do not need a car in Lisbon centre, there is a superbly integrated transport system encompassing underground, trams, buses and ferries. All can be paid for by using the Lisbon travel card, that can be topped up almost anywhere and if you are staying for more than a day or so, the travel card is well worth investing in.

The second point concerns general safety. Now as a couple of fifty somethings, we are not staying out all night drinking and having travelled all over the World, always keep our wits about us. However, to us Lisbon seems incredibly safe. We never once felt in any way threatened or unsafe despite travelling all over the city and beyond - literally

Following our visit to the ground of Sporting, it was time to do something that Lynda wanted to. We knew that not far outside Lisbon were a number of beach resort towns and one of the best reputed of these is Cascais. This small town is maybe 25 - 30 miles outside Lisbon. It is reached by an overland traditional railway, which departs the railway station at Cais Do Sodre, every 30 minutes or so. It seems to be a closed line with Lisbon centre and Cascais representing the two ends of the line. It cost around 5€ each way.

The train took around 35 minutes, with about four stops along the way. We found Cascais to be a very likeable resort, with some nice restaurants and bars. We had found in Porto that beaches situated close to cities were not always what they were cracked up to be in Portugal, but this was different. The beach at Cascais was great, clean, scenic uncrowded and with bars and restaurants at the back. In fact, there was more than one fine beach at Cascais, there were three. The town itself was touristy but in a nice way. All the shops were nicely set out and very local.

In Cascais, we were able to confirm something that we had long suspected - that the Portuguese were obsessed with sardines, particularly tinned sardines. They were for sale everywhere and there were even some shops that sold nothing else apart from tinned sardines. There was one such shop in Cascais and we decided that we would go inside in order to take a look.

We were shocked by what we found. Just about the smallest and cheapest tin of sardines was 5€ and the more expensive ones were over 50€. Quite what the difference was between a 5€ tin and a 50€ tin, we never did work out but, in any case, we passed on the deal. We prefer fresh sardines.

Whilst we did not actually see any British in Cascais, and certainly it does not seem to be on the main tourist trail, we guessed that they would have been there.

This was a tourist town and whilst it seemed primarily set up for domestic Portuguese tourists (nobody was advertising British or German food), the prices were higher even than Lisbon. However, there were a lot of positives to the resort - it was certainly not super exciting but excellent for a relaxing day or so.

We noticed that the train stop before Cascais, was Estoril, another tourist town. We did not get off at Estoril on this trip but vowed that we would do so the next time we visited.

One of the more touristy ways to get around Lisbon is by tram. There is a limited tram service that serves only a few parts of the city. It is almost exclusively used by tourists and is far too expensive for locals and so we were not really interested in travelling on a tourist tram.

However, the tram went up into the hills around the castle and close to the castle were the viewing platforms from which you got fantastic views over the city. We did not go into the castle, it did not seem worth it.

One of the supposed top tourist attractions in Lisbon is an old lift and viewing platform called the Elevator. It is actually located very close to where our hotel was - a few hundred yards along Av. Liberdade, at most. We have never been ones for organized tourism and so we did not go up the Elevator either. Whilst we were there, the queues were horrendous but to be honest we would not have paid to go up even had there been no queue.

We much preferred the terraces on the hills around the castle, where the views were spectacular and we could take them in whilst having a relaxing drink.

On the day before we were due to leave, we decided that we would visit the Estadio Da Luz, the Stadium of Light, the home ground of Benfica, Portugal's most famous and most successful football club. Even better, the ground was on the same underground line as was our hotel. We set off and reached the ground after about 15 minutes. The underground station serving the ground was in an enormous shopping centre across the road from the ground. We went over to the ground and as it was close to lunch, we found the stadium restaurant and went in for something to eat.

I think Benfica is my favourite ground in World football, it is a perfect bowl, so symmetrical and so colourful. The ground is so symmetrical, with its red seats and the three tiers separated by lines of smart looking executive boxes.

The club restaurant overlooks the ground and the views were spectacular - we spent most of our time taking photographs of the ground. There is a players' section to the restaurant - as we had discovered on a previous visit when we had tried to sit in there and had been moved - and there were people in there. Whether they were first team players, we could not tell, but it was good to tell ourselves that they were.

Prices in the restaurant were as you would expect - horrendous - 5€ for a small wine and 12€ for an individual pizza. However, the views and location made up for it.

After lunch we went back over to the shopping centre across the road and not fancying spending the rest of the day shopping, we decided to do something that we had never done in Portugal before. We decided that we would go to the Portuguese cinema.

We were spoiled for the choice of film. They were basically showing Hollywood films in English, with Portuguese sub-titles. I can't remember what we saw but it was not a blockbuster!! The seats were great, there were about five of us in the theatre and the seats were huge and mega comfortable. You could have slept in them.

At the end of the film, it was the end of our Lisbon trip. We went back to the hotel to pack and the following morning we would set off on our journey back. Lisbon had been fantastic.

We had been for a day trip previously but this time we really got to know the city. It had become one of our very favourites. We would definitely be back.

OIA

Following our stay in Lisbon, which was the furthest point from home of the whole trip, it was time to turn around and head on home. After the city centre of Lisbon and all of the things to do there, our next stop was Oia in the Galician province of northern Spain.

We had booked to stay in Budino De Serasecca, a very small Bed and Breakfast, that literally did seem to be in the absolute middle of nowhere. The journey down from Lisbon was about 250 miles and according to our sat nav it was going to take us around four and a half hours, without a stop.

We set out early in the morning and got out of Lisbon, before the main morning rush hour started. We found our way out of Lisbon fairly easily although there were precious few road signs.

Once out onto the motorway, it was a straight road heading due north, barely deviating from a straight line according to the map, following the west coast of the Iberian Peninsula all the way. I wish I could say that it was an interesting drive, but it was not. It was motorway and main road all the way and as we had been driving over here for over a month, the novelty value of driving in a different country had long since worn off.

When we got near to the property, around the town of Baiona it was clear that our sat nav was no longer going to be any help at all. Budino De serraseca did not even have a proper address and whilst its POSTAL address said Oia, we did not know where it was, but it definitely was not in Oia.

We were now in the hands of the directions which had been provided by the owners. As far as we could tell it was between Villadesousa and Mougas. It was not easy but we travelled through a couple of hamlets which were only just wide enough to fit our car through. In the end, as we approached the property, there were high green hedges on either side of us and it was difficult to know where we were or where we were going.

Eventually we arrived. It had taken hours. We were stiff from the journey but that did not take away from the first impression of the place. It was in the middle of incredibly scenic countryside. There were donkeys, dogs and chickens all amongst what seemed to be open countryside it was all as it should have been. The owners came out to see us. They did not speak a lot of English but made us very welcome. We were shown to our room and it was ok. A nice room in a country house.

We had paid 70€ per night for the room and breakfast for two. By that standard, it was a superb deal. By now we were pretty much well outside the prime months for tourists, and being well off the beaten track, we virtually had the place to ourselves for the five days that we were there. As we seemed effectively to be staying with a family in their private home, there was no prospect of getting anything for dinner, at the B&B and so, after we had unpacked again, we headed out to find something to eat.

By now it was getting dark. We asked the owners where the best place to go was, that was walkable. They pointed us to what seemed to be a local recreation club or social club that was around a mile away.

We set out and came across the small hamlet that we had passed through when approaching the property.

By now it was getting really dark and as we made our way past local homes, with high hedges when we heard the menacing growling of two very large sounding dogs. As we got nearer, we could make out their silhouettes and they were huge. More to the point they were not fenced in and occupied a position above us, where they could easily have jumped down onto us.

Whilst I am very wary of dogs, normally Lynda is not. This time however, she was as nervous as I was about these particular dogs. We edged past the dogs, our backs against the wall across the Lane from where they were positioned as far away as we could get.

They continued to bark but never did jump down. We carried on and eventually came to the bar/ restaurant that had been mentioned to us. It was very basic inside with lots of locals playing dominoes and cards. We sat outside, next to the main road through the village, although this was not a problem as there was no traffic.

The food and wine were very good and very cheap. They were not seeing many tourists out here, judging by the prices. It was around 1€ for a nice glass of local red wine and 5€ for a small fish main course. Whilst we visited this bar a few times, we never did quite work what the place actually was. It could have been some sort of non profit making community centre. Certainly, they were not making much profit at these prices.

Whilst we were able to take some very nice walks in the area around Budino' if truth be told, there was not a whole host of things to do in the area. This meant that unless we wanted to restrict our activities to walks and general relaxation, we were going to have to take the car and travel a bit further afield. The main town in the area was a very traditional Spanish seaside resort, by the name of Baiona.

Baiona was around 30 minutes from Budino. The first thing about Baiona we discovered was that even out of season, it has a parking problem. In the heart of town, there was just nowhere to park, so we had to go to a car park by the sea, outside the town and walk in. Not a problem because it was a nice walk - but this was not a particularly 'vehicle friendly' town.

Baiona is a great little seaside town, warm, busy, with great restaurants and local shopping, a nice harbour and as normal for northern Spain, spectacular beaches.

Probably Baiona's best claim to fame is that when Columbus sailed back from America in 1493, having discovered the New World, the Pinta, one of the two surviving ships actually sailed into Baiona harbour. So, Baiona was the first port to find out that Columbus' voyage had been a success.

To mark this piece of history, there is a life sized model of the Pinta in the harbour. It is only a couple of Euros to visit, and whilst we did not actually go aboard, we went to the far side of the harbour for a look.

What immediately occurred to us was how small the boat was. How on Earth two out of three ships of that size could make across the Atlantic and back is staggering. There were queues to get on the boat but being out of season, it was not too bad.

There seemed to be some sort of fort and historical type figures around the harbour. Clearly Baiona was a very important town in its day and has played its part in the history of Spain.

It would be wrong to describe Baiona as a tourist town, it is too far off the beaten path for that. However other than fishing, there did not seem to be any discernible way of making a living in the town other than tourism. However, it was domestic tourism, Spaniards visiting Spain. There were no foreigners that we could see, no restaurants pandering to English tastes, only Spanish chefs, looking after the Spanish tourists, in the main post ocho..

As I have said about most parts of northern Spain that we visited, there was a great atmosphere about the town. There was hustle and bustle but it was always pleasant. The bars and restaurants were very Spanish, some of them just peoples' living rooms and serving bits of ham and olives as tapas.

There were a few bigger restaurants and we took lunch in one. The prices were a bit higher than we were expecting but as we learned on this trip, if there is any possibility of a tourist euro, then the price's automatically go up. However, the prices were nothing like say the expensive bits of Cornwall.

When we are away, we like to see as much as we can of the local area and if there is not very much in the local area, we are always happy to travel a little further afield. This proved to be the case at Budino'. Basically, we ran out of things to do. Therefore, we decided that we would make day of it and go to Santiago De Compostella, the final stop on the Camino pilgrimage and allegedly the third most holy place in the Christian World and supposedly the burial site for the apostle, St James.

Santiago is about an hour and a half beyond Oia, going right into the top western corner of Spain. We had actually been once before and I have to say that on that visit we had been pretty disappointed.

However, we assumed that there must be a bit more to the place than we had seen previously and decided that we would give the place one more chance. We set off early in the morning, having taken a hearty country breakfast in Budino'. Parking was a problem, we just about got into a car park, right on the edge of town. By now we were into October and increasingly, rain was becoming a problem. It rained all the way to Santiago and continued to rain for most of the morning.

We must have looked bedraggled as we walked to the town square, under our brightly coloured ponchos. We reached the main square and found it just as we remembered it, a large square, surrounded by large and impressive stone churches and buildings. There were a lot of railings and crowd control barriers, funneling the crowds this way and that but to be truthful there were not really that many people in the square. In the early morning rain, it appeared to be a bit sad.

We went inside a few of the buildings and I have to say that one or two of them were a little atmospheric. However, over our substantial travels, we have visited a lot of churches and religious sites and almost all of them have been disappointing.

I am afraid that Santiago remained a disappointment to us. As I say one or two of the individual buildings had a feel to them, but the city itself is in no way a religious or holy place. It is exactly like Lourdes in

France is, an excuse for the locals to rip off pilgrims with every single type of fake religious artefact on sale at literally hundreds of shops and stalls, spread throughout the city.

I am afraid that the question we were left asking was how disappointed the pilgrims must be when they see what this place is like after they have walked the hundreds of miles of the Camino?

Perhaps that is unfair, perhaps we are missing the point but clearly, we do not get Santiago – that is why we gave it another chance. At such a holy site, we were expecting a religious experience, or at least a city that would impart a little calm in an otherwise crazy World. But it just is not like that. Just the same as many supposedly holy sites - it seemed to us to be all about the money. We get it that tourism is about the money but felt that perhaps religion should not be.

We returned to Budino' and went to our local community centre for dinner. The following day was to be our last and so we asked our property owner to suggest somewhere really nice for dinner on our last night. Not only did they know somewhere to go but also, they knew the owners and were able to book us in for the following night. We spent the next day, relaxing around the property and repacking for our next journey. We were ready well before the 7.30pm time we were booked in.

The restaurant was pretty much on its own, down on the sea front. When we had told the owner we wanted somewhere special, he had not let us down. The restaurant looked great and was a lot better than any other place we had visited. We were given a special table right at the front. I was driving as we would need to set off early the next day and so I was not able to drink too much. We both had the fish and it was superb. The prices were not too bad - particularly as the view we had from our table was one of the best we had ever seen.

The following day, we set off early as we had a long way to go. We had enjoyed our time at Budino', it had been very relaxing, but we had run out of things to do and places to see. Perhaps five days was stretching it at this location and three days would have been better.

BURGOS

By the time that our stopover in Oia was over, we were well into October and inevitably the weather in northern Spain was beginning to break down. We knew it would when we were booking this trip, and so we decided that for our penultimate stay in northern Spain, we would do something different.

We could have gone to Gijon, which was on our way, or to San Sebastián that was past Bilbao but the culinary capital of Spain. But no. We wanted to go to a bog standard, working Spanish city, with no tourists, in order to see how your ordinary Spanish city dweller was living.

In order to ensure that there were no tourists, we had to stay away from the coast and well away from anything that might draw in numbers of tourists. In northern Spain, that is no easy task, but we did our homework and the nearest thing that we could come up with was the city of Burgos, in the province of the same name.

It was a long way from Oia but when you are planning these trips, the distances do not seem real. When you say that you might have to drive for five and a half hours, when you are sat in the lounge at home, pre trip, it does not sound too bad. When you are sat in your car in Oia at the start of a journey that will take five hours without a stop, if was pretty daunting.

The positive was that we had all day to get there and could share the driving if things got too bad. The route taken by our sat nav took us right across country, staying away from the coast. Our first marker along the way was Ourense, then we headed out to the outskirts of Leon and then down to Burgos.

We went right through the heart of northern Spain. The scenery was green and mountainous. We went over rivers, through valleys and past small villages and towns. We stayed on the main roads, which were in places single track - there was some dual carriageway but no motorway.

In the end the journey took a total of seven hours, with a couple of short stops included. We would have had one of the ridiculously cheap menu Del Dias at one of the small country restaurants we passed but we didn't have the time for a two hour lunch.

So, it was a bocadillo and drink as we were travelling. Lynda did a stint of driving, whilst I had my sandwich. We felt that this journey gave us more of a realistic impression of Spanish country life, than any other journey, which we took on this trip.

We arrived at the Puerto De Burgos Hotel just after 3pm. We were only staying for three nights and so it was important that the hotel had secure parking, so that we did not have to unpack two months' worth of clothes for a three night stay. We could not actually find the car park and so parked in front of reception, whilst we checked in and asked about car parking.

We had booked a top floor suite at the hotel, which without breakfast cost the incredibly reasonable 65€ per night. However on to that needed to be added the 8€ per night for secure parking.

It turned out that the car park was underground, actually beneath the hotel. The entrance to the car park was automatic and was located at the rear of the hotel. In common with nearly all similar car parks in Spain, the entrance to it was tight and the spaces were incredibly tight. However, we were the only ones in the car park, and so we parked across two spaces. We grabbed the overnight bags we had prepared for this short stay but left the majority of our clothes in our car.

We went up to our top floor suite and to be honest could not believe it. The room was well appointed, modern and huge. There were fantastic views over the city and a river, which ran through the city. How this room could be priced at only 65€ was beyond us. It was getting toward early evening by now and after the ten minutes or so it took us to unpack our overnight bag, we headed out to get something to eat and to walk some blood back into our legs, following the long journey.

We headed out and were immediately pleased that we had paid for secure parking. Whilst, by UK standards the area was fine, by Spanish standards this seemed to be a less than perfect area. There was nothing we could put our finger on, but the hotel seemed to be located in a slightly rough area. We walked along a huge tree lined avenue, into the centre of town. As we walked further toward the centre of the city, the area got brighter and the place got busier. As in most of Spain, it seemed that the later it got, the busier it became.

As we approached the town centre it had become dark and so there was no point in any sightseeing. The shops were all still open, but we did not fancy doing that, so we flopped down in the first traditional tapas bar that we came to and stayed there for the night. We knew that the ordinary restaurants would not start serving dinner until ocho and so we decided that we would have tapas (which you could have at any time) and wine for dinner, together with a piece of fruit, from the stash we had brought with us, when we got back to the room.

The tapas was great, prawn, cod, cheese and sardine on small sections of bread, heated or not. The tapas was 1€ a piece and the wine 1.25€. After 3 tapas and a couple of wines, we had had our fill and after such a long journey, we were falling asleep and so set off back to the hotel. Somehow, after two wines, the area around the hotel looked better in the dark. We slept very well that night.

The following morning, we were up and out early. Breakfast in the hotel was going to cost 8€ and so we went into town to take breakfast with the locals. We found the smallest, dingiest, most local looking bar in the area and went inside to join the throng.

We found a table and sat down. We sat there for a short while and eventually realised that there was no table service in this bar. Lynda did not fancy going up to the bar and so I was volunteered to join the throng waiting to be served.

I ordered two coffees and two tostado y tomates- the bill was less than 4€ - we were going to like it here. The coffee and tomato toast was superb - no wonder it was so busy in here. After breakfast, we carried on into town. At the end of the road, which ran just outside our hotel, was the town centre and a large square.

Whilst our stay to date had told us that this was a working city, there did seem to be a few tourists around the town square and no wonder. The square was full of important looking buildings and beneath the pillars of these buildings there were odd stalls selling bric a brac, umbrellas and tourist goods. Presumably, there would be a weekly market in this same square, but it did not happen, whilst we were there.

We later found out that the main building we had looked at was Burgos cathedral. After a couple of hours looking around, we went to find the local food market. In Spain, it is always worth searching out the local food market, we always find it interesting how appetising Spanish fruit and veg looks in the markets, compared to how dank and uninteresting that UK supermarkets manage to make fruit and veg look.

After asking only a couple of people in our pigeon Spanish we managed to understand that 'el mercado Norte municipal' (North public market) was where we needed to be.

Our Spanish was not good enough to take full directions and the market seemed to be a fair way away. So, we jumped into a taxi and about 5 minutes later we were dropped at the market. It was a fair size, with dozens of stall holders, each seemingly selling produce that they personally or somebody they knew had grown. It was around harvest festival time when we visited and the selection of fruits was incredible. Surely, they were physically polishing the apples, the shine on them could not be natural.

The clientele at the market and the stall holders themselves looked exactly like each other, followed exactly the same demographic and could have changed groups, without anybody noticing. There were no youngsters in the market, very few males and nobody who seemed to be aged under 45. There were lots of stern looking Spanish ladies, many in headscarves, shopping for the family in the same way that they had for years if not decades before.

We speculated that the younger element were either at work or had foresaken the traditional markets for the convenience of supermarkets.

After around an hour in the market, we took one of the taxis, which were waiting outside, to get back to the hotel. It did not take long to get back to the hotel, we could have walked but as we had got to the market by taxi, we didn't really know the way back. That night we ate in the hotel. It was a fixed menu, with three courses, for 15€, this is a lot for dinner in northern Spain, but that particular meal had been well worth it.

We liked Burgos, it could best be summed up by the phrase 'working class'. None of the restaurants nor bars had a hint of pretension, none pandered to tourists, even though there were some tourists around. The shopping was the same, whilst there was the odd luxury goods shop, so that the locals could treat themselves, when they felt like it, the majority of the shopping was functional and local. There were department stores, but these sold cheaper end goods and clothing.

The people seemed to be hardworking and friendly. There was none of the people hanging around, that you see in the Mediterranean areas. Everybody seemed busy and had somewhere to go.

The traffic was busy and the weather was British, wet and pretty miserable whilst we were there. The three days we had allowed for the trip was perfect for this city. After the first full day we spent there, we had basically exhausted most of the things that there were to do and for the second and third days, we were there we found ourselves repeating what we had done on the first day.

However, we had been able to get to know the city in a way we would not, had we been dashing from one sight to the next and felt that it had been worth the days we had spent in the city, if only for that.

During our time in Burgos, it had been dull and rainy for almost the whole of the three days we had been there. As the final week and a bit was to be spent at Noja, which is essentially a seaside resort, close to Santander, we sincerely hoped that it would clear up!!

NOJA

The very final stop of our northern Spain and Portugal trip was to be the small town of Noja on the North coast, situated between the major cities of Santander and Bilbao. It was a town we had previously spent a night or so at, prior to a ferry departure back to the UK. Both times we had been, we had stayed only for a day or so and we always said that had been a great shame. Therefore, on this occasion we had decided to stay for a full eight days to get a real feel for the town and the area.

It was by the time we arrived in Noja mid to late October and so we were taking a real chance with the weather. We would however still have the car and so if it did rain, we could go and see what else was in the area. Indeed, 8 days would be too long to stay in a town the size of Noja and so we were going to have to get out and about in any case.

For the three days we had been in Burgos, the weather in northern Spain had started to break down and we had experienced three days of rain and dullness. If our eight days in Noja were going to be like this, then that was going to be a problem.

The day we left Burgos, the weather turned. It was only about a two and a half hour drive to Noja so we were able to have a leisurely breakfast in the hotel and to delay our departure until approx 11am, which was the time we were required to check out, in any case.

The journey was uneventful and before we knew it, we were approaching the small town of Noja. It looked exactly as we had remembered it. We were to stay at a small B&B, which we had seen on our previous visit, called Posada Da Mies. We had booked a junior suite, in the hotel, which was not actually on the coast but within half a mile of the town's spectacular beach. Noja is not the easiest place in the World to navigate, despite its small size and it took us a good 20 minutes to find the place, after we had reached Noja.

When we reached the hotel, the first thing that struck us was something that we had not thought about when we had seen it, but not stayed, on our previous visit. There was no hotel parking. Whilst there were a couple of parking spots, situated right in front of the hotel, they were taken, and we had to find a parking spot away from the hotel. We sincerely hoped that parking was not going to be a problem that would dog the final few days of the trip. We parked up and rang the doorbell. The owner came to the door. It was like a very large house.

We were welcomed, checked in and were shown our room, it was large and well appointed. The wi-fi signal was excellent and we had a small balcony, overlooking the square below. We spoke to the owners about the parking for the hotel and our fears were realised. The hotel had no designated parking, we had to take our chances in the public on-street parking, outside the hotel.

However, one crumb of comfort was offered, the area was safe, and as it was outside the prime season, we would always be able to find somewhere. In peak season, even finding a parking spot is apparently a nightmare. However, for the 65€ per night we had paid, it was an incredible bargain.

It was clear that we could not leave anything in the car overnight, and so we got everything out of the car and into our room. It took quite a while, but we knew that at the end of our hard work we would be able to go down to the beach to recharge our batteries. It took us about 20 minutes of ferrying things to the car and then something marvelous happened. One of the cars parked right next to our hotel moved and so we immediately took the open spot. It made the ferrying of belongings that much easier.

After we had finished the carrying, without unpacking we put our swimming gear on beneath our clothes and headed out. Lynda remarked that our room looked as though a bomb had hit it - but we would sort it out when we got back.

We walked the half a mile or so to the beach. For anybody who has not seen the beach at Noja, your first view is one that you will never forget. The bay is a perfect semi circle and at high tide, there would be nothing to see, other than the fantastic beach itself.

However, as the tide goes out, a different world is revealed. Bit by bit, large free standing, limestone 'karsks' are revealed. They are like hundreds of stone statues, jutting out of the sand or sea. It is incredibly scenic and how this place is not on everybody's bucket list is beyond me.

As we walked down to the beach the temperature must have been in the mid to late seventies. Perfect temperature for sitting and relaxing. We found a suitable spot, which was not difficult bearing in mind that there were probably less than 20 people on this whole sweeping beach.

It was a bit windy but really pleasant, we were going to enjoy it here. We knew what the sea would be like but ever the optimist I went down to the waters' edge for a paddle. Yep - it was absolutely freezing. We were going to have to build ourselves up for any attempted swim in the sea.

We stayed on the beach for a good couple of hours and after the heat had started to go out of the day, we headed back to the hotel to sort out the room and indeed sort ourselves out, before going out for dinner. We knew that the watershed of ocho would apply and so there was no point in rushing. A few hours later we were ready, the room looked fine, we had bathed in the rather antiquated but perfectly adequate bathroom. We knew where to head and went to the town centre.

This late in the season, there were not many tourists around, but all of the locals and their offspring come out in the evening to eat and drink, whilst the kids play football or on the play equipment at one end of the square. There were bars and restaurants on the outside of the square and there were seats and tables set up toward the centre of the square.

We chose a suitable restaurant and settled in for a few drinks and a good meal. The prices in Noja were basically tourist prices - 2.50€ for a wine and 12€ for a main course. However as everywhere else we had encountered in Spain, the food and wine were excellent.

We zig-zagged our way back to our hotel having had one too many wines each and slept very soundly. The following morning, we took our breakfast in the town centre. We decided to have the typical Spanish breakfast of churros, which are essentially long strands of doughnut, which are dipped in chocolate.

It is really good but not particularly healthy - so best not to have it every day. As our second day was again sunny and warm, we decided to make hay, whilst the sun shines and visit the beach again.

Lynda has an almost unquenchable appetite for lying on beaches, if it were an Olympic sport then she would be a medal prospect. On the other hand, I am ok sitting on the beach for a while, but with a low boredom threshold, I have to mix it with activity. The sea was too cold to regularly swim in and so I would take a walk going into town and have a look round and just take in the scenery not only on the beach but in town also. I would also stop at the odd coffee shop and sample a little local cake and the local coffee.

For about three days our lives went on like this, the weather held and so we stayed on the spectacular beach and generally stayed local. This on the basis that sooner or later the weather was going to start getting worse and we would be prevented from going to the beach then, so we may as well go now.

Eventually, around half way through our eight day stay, the weather did break. We awoke to a dull, slightly damp and much colder day. We decided that we would go out for the day.

Isla is just about the closest neighbouring town to Noja and is almost walkable. It took us about five minutes to drive to Isla town centre. It seemed to be a rather downmarket town, compared to Noja. The whole town is located along a series of beaches.

There are hotels, restaurants and bars throughout the town. Isla was one of those places that seemed like it would not be where it was if it was not for the tourist dollar. The problem with towns like Isla is that when the tourists have gone, there is nothing left. When we went - which was admittedly well out of season - there was nobody around.

We did not spend a great deal of time at Isla and decided to visit Santona, a small town on the other side of Noja, from Isla.

Santona was a proper Spanish seaside town. Whilst there were beaches and a promenade along one of the particularly long beaches, this was a vibrant varied town. Whilst there were tourists around, this was not a town, which was wholly reliant on tourists.

There was an infrastructure and busy nature to the town, which made it pleasant to visit and explore.

it is famous for its anchovies and weirdly there is a statue to anchovies, near to the sea front. The promenade shows evidence of a Virgin Mary statue and there are lots of statues and art, all along the promenade. We were able to select a sea front restaurant for lunch and had to try the anchovies, which were 5€ for a relatively large portion. Prices were low generally, all around town. After spending the day or at least the afternoon, wandering around, we returned to Noja and as usual headed into the town centre to take dinner. It had been a great day.

The remaining days of our trip to Noja were favoured by good weather, and so as we had done a great deal of travelling over the last two months, we decided that we would leave the car and explore Noja on foot.

Each day, Lynda would spend some of the day on the beach and then we would go for walks, exploring both ends of the beach and walking the north Spanish coastal path, which runs from Noja out towards the Isla direction. The path was so scenic, running along the rocky coast.

We never did get used to the unbelievable scenery of Noja beach - seriously google it, to me it seems incredible that Noja beach is not listed amongst the most scenic on the planet. We have visited over 90 countries in the World and it is one of the best we have seen.

We ate out every day and tried to spread our business around to a number of different bars and restaurants. I normally do not like doing this, often I will pick a place and try to stick with it. Lynda however likes to try a whole host of different places and as ever she won out.

Whilst on the subject of eating we have to mention the two bakery shops in Noja town centre. They are excellent quality and their cakes absolutely superb – if a little expensive, even by tourist standards.

Before we knew it our time in Noja was up and we were back in our room packing for the last time in readiness for our departure. It had been a brilliant end to a brilliant trip. Whilst we had not ventured out from Noja as much as we might have, we had really gotten to know this little town really well.

We had intended to go to a fancy restaurant for the last night of the trip - but there really are not that many fancy restaurants in Noja and so we simply chose one of those restaurants, we had visited before. Over dinner we were already discussing when we would return.

JOURNEY HOME & FINAL THOUGHTS

Our ferry back to the UK meant an early start but at least this was a direct, rather than economie voyage and so there was only one night on the boat rather than two. When we left Posada De Mies it was still dark and we made our way to the port of Bilbao along the northern coast road that we had travelled, in the opposite direction, only two months before. To be honest it seemed like two years before.

We reached the port around two hours and thirty minutes before departure time. We were told that the ferry was on time and so having picked up our room key and documents we made our way into the holding car park, prior to embarkation. As we were so early, the bar/ restaurant in the port, which has 2 staff to serve about 500 passengers and is normally swamped was empty. We got two cheese toastie and two coffees. Not long after we arrived in the port, the ferry we would be leaving on arrived.

We watched the boat disembark its passengers and eventually it was emptied and our embarkation began. It was over. In two days time, we would be back in the UK, preparing for the winter. We had enjoyed every minute but now it was over.

Northern Spain - wow. What a region. Every tiny little town and village that you have never even heard of, has a beach better than any in Cornwall. There are mountains, valleys, rivers and the some of the most lush forests you have ever seen.

All this against a background of friendly people, brilliant food and drink, superb accommodation and fantastic prices. It could be summed up as Cornwall with low prices and good beaches. One day this will be a major holiday area, not just for the Spanish - but for the rest of Europe.

The ONLY potential downsides are that there is only one ferry operator to this area, Brittany Ferries, a French company that does not always cover itself in glory and the weather, which outside of July and August can be sketchy.

Otherwise - what a region.

Printed in Great Britain
by Amazon

85844893R00068